DOMINICAN REPUBLIC

A TRUE BOOK

by
Elaine Landau

Children's Press®
A Division of Grolier Publishing

New York London Hong Kong Sydney
Danbury, Connecticut

Lake Enriquillo

Reading Consultant
Linda Cornwell
*Coordinator of School Quality
and Professional Improvement
Indiana State Teachers
Association*

Author's Dedication
For Derek Kessler

Visit Children's Press® on the
Internet at:
http://publishing.grolier.com

Library of Congress Cataloging-in-Publication Data

The Dominican Republic / by Elaine Landau.
    P.   cm.—(A true book)
Includes bibliographical references.
Summary: A basic overview of the history, geography, climate, and cul-
ture of the Dominican Republic.
    ISBN: 0-516-21171-4 (lib. bdg.)   0-516-27022-2 (pbk.)
    1. Dominican Republic—Juvenile literature.   [1. Dominican Republic.]
I. Title.   II. Series
F1934.2.L26 2000
972.93—dc21
                                                                99-13663
                                                                CIP
                                                                AC

GROLIER
PUBLISHING

1 2 3 4 5 6 7 8 9 10 R 09 08 07 06 05 04 03 02 01 00

Contents

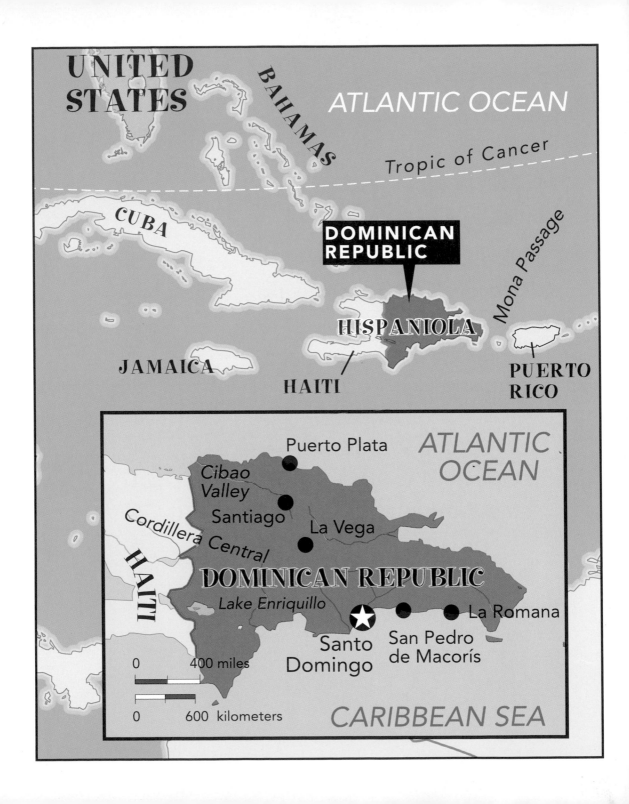

The Dominican Republic

The Dominican Republic is a country in the West Indies covering 18,816 square miles (48,734 square kilometers). The country occupies more than half of the eastern area of the island of Hispaniola. The western area is the country of Haiti.

Hispaniola lies about 600 miles (965 kilometers) southeast of Miami, Florida. The Caribbean Sea lies on the south side of the island and the Atlantic Ocean is to its north. A 75-mile (121-km)-wide channel known as the Mona Passage separates the Dominican Republic from Puerto Rico. The Dominican Republic is the second-largest country in the West Indies after Cuba.

The Cordillera Central is the largest mountain chain of the island.

Geographically, the Dominican Republic is a land of many faces. The Cordillera Central (Central Mountains) runs from the north-west to the southeast through the center of the island. It includes Duarte Peak, the highest peak in the West Indies. It is 10,417 feet (3,175 meters) above sea level. Smaller mountain ranges rise along the country's northern coast and in the southwest.

Four major rivers, along with many smaller ones, flow down from the mountains to the ocean and sea. Lake Enriquillo, in the west, is the largest lake in the Caribbean. It is about 125 square miles (201 sq km). A small island in the center of the lake is home to the world's

The American crocodile (above) and the rhinoceros iguana (right) are two of the many reptiles found on Lake Enriquillo.

largest surviving population of American crocodiles. The endangered rhinoceros iguana and several types of endangered turtles are also found there.

The Cibao Valley in the north is the Dominican Republic's largest and most important valley. It includes the Vega Real (Royal Plain), which is sometimes called the Garden of the Caribbean. Its rich soil makes this plain one of the country's most fertile spots. Various fruits, vegetables, and sugarcane are grown there. The Vega Real also has excellent grazing pastures.

The National Palace in Santo Domingo

The Dominican Republic's capital, Santo Domingo, and its major ports are on the southern coast. Uncharted coral reefs and grasslands are found on the country's small offshore islands.

A Tropical Climate

A typical summer day

Temperatures in the Dominican Republic range from 73° Fahrenheit (23° Celsius) in the winter to 82° F (28° C) in the summer. August is the hottest month on the island, and January is the coldest. In the mountains, however, the temperature can drop to as low as 30° F (-1° C).

Flowering amapola trees

During the months of August and September, the island experiences occasional destructive hurricanes. In 1998, Hurricane Georges struck the island, killing more than two hundred people.

A stormy day on the island

History and Government

Hispaniola was Spain's first colony in the New World. Christopher Columbus, who arrived there on December 6, 1492, was the first European to set foot on the island.

As the years passed, large numbers of Spanish colonists settled in Hispaniola. The

Columbus arriving in
Hispaniola, in 1492

Spaniards enslaved the
American Indians already living
there. Often they were starved
and brutally beaten. Many died
from the cruel treatment, and

others died from diseases brought by the Spanish.

Spaniards often came to the Dominican Republic in search of gold. Many left when they didn't strike it rich. With only a small number of settlers scattered along the coast, Spanish trading vessels rarely stopped there. As a result, the settlers were often attacked by pirates. In the 1600s, Spain ordered all its colonists to stay close to Santo Domingo for protection.

Soon, French settlers moved into the regions the Spanish colonists had abandoned and other parts of the island. In 1697, by the Treaty of Ryswick,

Spain was forced to recognize France's claims to the western area of the island.

In time, the island's boundaries changed again. The African slaves who had been brought to Haiti revolted and took over the entire island. France and Spain fought to regain their colonies, but they only managed to do so for short periods.

In 1821, the Spanish colony declared its independence

from Spain, but its freedom was short-lived. Weeks later, the Haitians again seized control of the entire island, calling it Estado Independiente del Haití Español (Independent State of Spanish Haiti).

In 1844, while he was in exile, Juan Pablo Duarte led a successful revolt against the Haitians and established the Dominican Republic as an independent nation. But even then, Dominicans weren't given true freedom. Over the years, a series of dictators seized power and the people had only brief periods of democratic rule. During violent upheavals from 1916 to 1924 and from 1965 to 1966, United States troops were sent to the Dominican Republic to try and prevent bloodshed.

Today, the president of the Dominican Republic is Leonel Fernández Reyna, who was elected to office in 1996. The

Leonel Fernández Reyna (left) was elected president of the Dominican Republic in 1996.

Dominican Republic's constitution provides for the election of a president and congressional representatives. A judicial branch of the government handles the court system and legal issues.

The People

The people of the Dominican Republic today are a blend of those who lived there in the past. As a result, the Dominican Republic is a multicultural nation with a distinctly Spanish flavor.

Spanish is the country's official language. More than half

People of the
Dominican Republic

of the nation's eight million people have mixed Spanish and African ancestry. Contact with Haiti has somewhat influenced Dominican culture. But the African influence in Dominican culture comes from the thousands of slaves who were brought to the island by the Spanish.

Some Dominicans are Caucasian, meaning white or European. There are small groups of European Jews and

Asians. Very few individuals are descended from the natives who once lived in the Dominican Republic. They were almost wiped out by Spanish colonists.

Many of the people living in rural areas of the Dominican Republic are farm- ers. Some own small farms where they grow enough food for their families and sell some crops to buy necessary items. Haitians work on large

A sugarcane field in Puerto Plata

sugar plantations for low wages. Often, farm families in the Dominican Republic live in small shacks with thatched roofs and dirt floors. The government is gradually replacing these homes with better buildings.

Dominicans who live in cities are employed in factories, businesses, and government offices. In the 1970s and 1980s, many Dominicans moved to Santo Domingo

New government housing projects (background) are replacing older, rundown homes (foreground).

and other urban centers to look for work. City people often live in apartments.

Children in the Dominican Republic must attend school from ages seven to fourteen, but many don't go past elementary school. Public school is free, but in many areas there are not enough schools and teachers. Some cities do have private and religious schools. After graduation, some young people go on to one of the

Dominican Republic's colleges to study medicine, marine biology, business, art, or music. Dominicans enjoy many outdoor activities. Baseball (or

Dominican players warming up before a baseball game

pelota) is the national sport, and the country has produced several of today's outstanding U.S. superstars, such as Sammy Sosa, Pedro Martínez, and Manny Ramírez. Basketball, tennis, and football are also popular sports on the island.

Most people in the Dominican Republic are Roman Catholic. Near the Haitian border, some religious groups practice voodoo religions based on African traditions.

Home-Run Hero

A native of San Pedro de Marcorís, Sammy Sosa is one of the most famous Dominicans in the world. Sammy was already a star Chicago Cubs baseball player before the 1998 season. But in that year, he captured the love of fans across America when he dueled St. Louis Cardinals slugger Mark McGwire for baseball's home-run record. They both wound up breaking the single-season record of sixty-one homers. Sammy hit sixty-six and McGwire hit seventy. Today, Sammy keeps on slugging and bringing smiles to baseball fans everywhere.

The Economy

The Dominican Republic's economy depends on agriculture. Sugar is the country's most valuable export crop. Coffee, cocoa beans, and tobacco are also important. Many farmers grow rice, corn, beans, tomatoes, and plantains (a banana-like fruit).

Beans (above) and tomatoes (left) are two important crops to the Dominican economy.

Mining is also important in the Dominican Republic. It is the second-largest gold producer in the Western Hemisphere. The country has silver, nickel, tin, marble, and limestone, as well.

Much of the nation's industry, such as sugar refining and metal processing, is based on its natural resources. Other manufactured items include processed foods, cement, textiles, and wood products.

Many Haitians work in the sugarcane fields.

In recent years, the government has tried to promote tourism. It has also encouraged foreign businesses to relocate to the Dominican Republic.

Art and Culture

When some people think of the Dominican Republic's art and culture, they think of music. Dominican folk music combines Latin and African rhythms. It is popular throughout the country. Dominicans also enjoy dancing. The national dance is the merengue.

A merengue festival

Several outstanding poets and novelists come from the Dominican Republic. They include: Gastón Fernando Deligne and Salomé Ureña de Henríquez. Book clubs are common in many regions. Joaquín Balaguer and Juan Bosch Gaviño not only were Dominican presidents, but they are famous writers as well. In addition, Dominican craftspeople are known for their fine wood carvings and silver and amber jewelry.

A statue of Christopher Columbus stands in front of the Cathedral of Santa María.

The Dominican Republic has several important historical sites. Some historians believe that Christopher Columbus is buried in the Cathedral of Santa María, in Santo Domingo. Santo

Domingo is the oldest capital in North America.

The Zona Colonial (Colonial Zone) in Santo Domingo has been described as a living history lesson. Most of the buildings there look just as they did five hundred years ago. Today these buildings serve as the country's museums and art galleries.

The Dominican Republic has much for visitors to see and enjoy. Besides its rugged mountainous beauty and white sandy

Many tourists are drawn to the beautiful Dominican beaches.

beaches, the country is steeped in history. At one time the Dominican Republic was the gateway to the New World. Now its culture offers a rich mix of the past and the present.

To Find Out More

Here are some additional resources to help you learn more about the Dominican Republic:

 **Books**

Anderson, Joan. **Christopher Columbus: From Vision to Voyage.** Dial Books For Young Readers, 1991.

Black, Eric. **Haiti: Land of Inequality.** Lerner Publishing, 1998.

Dwyer. Christopher. **Dominican Americans.** Chelsea House, 1991.

Haverstock, Nathan A. **Dominican Republic in Pictures.** Lerner Publishing, 1993.

MacLean, Caleb. **Sammy Sosa.** Children's Press, 1999.

ESPN / Sammy Sosa Profile
http://espn.go.com/mlb/ profiles/profile/4344.html

Maintained by ESPN Sports, this site features Sammy Sosa's player profile, statistics, scouting report, career notes, and much more.

History of Dance / Merengue
http://www.centralhome. com/ballroomcountry/ history.htm

Learn all about the national dance of the Dominican Republic. This site provides fun information on the history of the merengue and dozens of other dances.

Marine Mammals Sanctuary of the Dominican Republic
http://www.civila.com/ jorobada/index-eng.htm

Read about the sanctuary dedicated to promoting, educating, and supporting the preservation of the environment and the endangered species found in the Dominican Republic.

Santo Domingo
http://www.dominicana. com.do/english/engsd.htm

Maintained by the Minister of Tourism, this site features pictures of Santo Domingo and other Dominican cities. It also provides helpful information about the island's culture, historical landmarks, geography, and people.

Surfing the Net With Kids/ The Best Columbus Sites
http://www.surfnetkids.com/ columbus.htm

This site provides a listing of the best online sites available for kids about Christopher Columbus.

United Nations Cyber School Bus
One United Nations Plaza
Room DC1-552
New York, NY 10017
http://www.un.org/Pubs/ CyberSchoolBus

This site takes visitors to countries all over the world. Play games, look at flags, and find facts about the Dominican Republic and other countries.

45

Important Words

agriculture farming

channel a narrow stretch of water between two land areas

constitution the basic laws and practices that govern a country

dictator someone who has total control of a country

exile the state of being forced to leave one's home or country

pasture grazing ground for animals

rural having to do with the countryside

seize to take or grab

urban having to do with the city or city life

voodoo a religion based on African beliefs

Index

(**Boldface** page numbers indicate illustrations.)

Meet the Author

Popular author Elaine Landau worked as a newspaper reporter, editor, and a youth services librarian before becoming a full-time writer. She has written more than one hundred nonfiction books for young people, including many books for Franklin Watts and Children's Press. Ms. Landau, who has a bachelor's degree in English and journalism from New York University and a master's degree in library and information science from Pratt Institute, lives in Miami, Florida, with her husband and son.